I0504724

"A guide on building a thriving YouTube channel."

Introduction

Welcome to "A Guide to Building a Thriving YouTube Channel." This ebook is designed to help you create a successful YouTube channel that can attract a loyal following and generate revenue.

YouTube has become one of the most popular platforms for sharing video content, and it offers tremendous opportunities for those who want to create engaging and informative content. However, building a successful channel can be challenging and requires dedication, hard work, and strategic planning.

In this ebook, we will walk you through creating a successful YouTube channel step-by-step. We will cover everything from choosing the right niche to creating engaging content, optimizing your videos for search engines, building a loyal fanbase, and monetizing your channel.

We will also provide tips and tricks to help you stay ahead of the competition and grow your channel faster. Whether you are a beginner who is just starting out or an experienced YouTuber who wants to take your channel to the next level, this ebook has something for everyone.

So, if you are ready to build a thriving YouTube channel and achieve your goals, let's get started!

Index

- Choose a niche that you are passionate about and that has the potential for growth.
- Create high-quality, engaging content that stands out from the crowd.
- Be consistent with your upload schedule, so your viewers know when to expect new content.
- Optimize your videos for search engines by using relevant keywords and tags.
- Collaborate with other YouTubers in your niche to reach a wider audience.
- Promote your videos on social media and other platforms to increase visibility.
- Encourage your viewers to like, comment, and share your videos to help them reach more people.
- Engage with your audience by responding to comments and messages, and listening to their feedback.
- Use eye-catching thumbnails and titles to attract viewers and entice them to click on your videos.

- Stay up-to-date with trends and changes in the YouTube algorithm to stay ahead of the competition.
- Build a strong brand identity and use it consistently across all your social media platforms.
- Use analytics to track your performance and make data-driven decisions to improve your channel.
- Experiment with different types of content to see what resonates with your audience.
- Create a community around your channel by hosting live streams and interacting with your viewers in real time.
- Monetize your channel by joining the YouTube Partner Program, selling merchandise, or partnering with sponsors.

Chapter-1

Choose a niche that you are passionate about
And that has the potential for growth.

Choosing the right niche is crucial for building a succ essful YouTube channel. It is important to choose a topic that you are passionate about and knowledgeable in, as this will help you create high-quality, engaging content that resonates with your audience. Additionally, it is important to choose a niche that has potential for growth, so that you can attract new viewers and expand your channel over time.

When choosing a niche, it is important to consider your interests and skills. You should choose a topic that you enjoy talking about and that you are knowledgeable about, as this will make it easier for you to create engaging content that stands out from the crowd. Additionally, it is important to consider your target audience and their interests. You should choose a niche that has a large and engaged audience, as this will help you attract new viewers and build a loyal following.

To find the right niche, it can be helpful to do some research. You should look at popular YouTube channels in your area of interest and see what types of content they are creating. Additionally, you can use keyword research tools to see what people are searching for online, and use this information to guide your content creation.

Once you have chosen a niche, it is important to stay focused on your topic and create content that is relevant to your audience. This will help you build a loyal following and establish yourself as an authority in your niche. Additionally, you should be open to feedback from your viewers and be willing to make adjustments to your content to better serve their needs.

It is also important to consider the potential for growth when choosing a niche. You should choose a topic that has room for expansion so that you can attract new viewers and expand your channel over time. This can be achieved by exploring different subtopics within your niche, collaborating with other creators, and experimenting with new types of content.

Overall, choosing the right niche is essential for building a successful YouTube channel. By choosing a topic that you are passionate about and that has potential for growth, you can create engaging content that resonates with your audience and attracts new viewers over time.

Chapter-2

Create high-quality, engaging content that stands out from the crowd.

Creating high-quality, engaging content is key to building a successful YouTube channel. Your content should stand out from the crowd and capture the attention of your audience, encouraging them to watch, like, comment and share your videos.

One of the most important things to consider when creating content is your target audience. You should create content that speaks to their interests, needs, and preferences. This requires a deep understanding of your audience and what motivates them to watch YouTube videos. You can use analytics and feedback to gather insights about your viewers and adjust your content strategy accordingly.

Another important aspect of creating high-quality content is production value. Your videos should be well-shot, well-lit, and have good sound quality. This can be achieved with basic equipment such as a good-quality camera and microphone. It is important to make sure that your videos are visually appealing and engaging so that your audience is captivated from the beginning.

In addition to production value, the content itself should be informative, entertaining, and engaging. You should aim to create videos that are both educational and entertaining, providing value to your viewers while keeping them entertained. This can be achieved through creative storytelling, humor, and engaging visuals.

It is also important to be consistent with your content production. You should set a schedule for your videos and stick to it so that your viewers know when to expect new content from you. This helps to build a loyal following and ensures that your channel stays top of mind.

In order to stand out from the crowd, it is important to bring a unique perspective to your content. You should strive to create videos that are different from what others are creating, and that showcase your personality and style. This will help you build a strong brand identity and attract a loyal following.

Another important aspect of creating engaging content is to keep up with the latest trends and topics in your niche. You should be aware of what your competitors are doing and stay up to date with new developments in your field. This will help you stay relevant and ensure that your content remains fresh and interesting.

Finally, it is important to be open to feedback from your audience. You should encourage your viewers to leave comments and feedback on your videos and take this feedback into account when creating new content. This will help you improve the quality of your videos and build a stronger connection with your audience.

In summary, creating high-quality, engaging content requires a deep understanding of your target audience, good production value, creativity, consistency, a unique perspective, staying up to date with trends and topics, and being open to feedback. By focusing on these elements, you can create videos that stand out from the crowd and build a successful YouTube channel.

Chapter-3

Be consistent with your upload schedule, so your viewers know when to expect new content.

Consistency is key to building a successful YouTube channel. By establishing a regular upload schedule, you can build a loyal following and ensure that your viewers know when to expect new content from you. This can help to increase engagement, views, and subscribers. One of the most important aspects of consistency is creating a regular upload schedule. You should decide how often you want to post new videos and stick to that schedule. This can be once a week, twice a week, or any other frequency that you feel comfortable with. By creating a regular schedule, you can train your viewers to expect new content from you at specific times.

In addition to a regular upload schedule, it is important to maintain consistency in the quality and format of your videos. Your viewers should be able to recognize your brand and style and feel confident that they will receive the same high-quality content with every new video. This can help to build trust and loyalty with your audience. Another way to maintain consistency is by using a template or format for your videos. This can include a standard intro and outro, consistent branding elements, and a recognizable visual style. By using a template, you can streamline your video production process and ensure that your videos are consistent in terms of branding and format.

It is also important to engage with your viewers on a regular basis. This can be through comments, social media, or other forms of communication. By engaging with your audience, you can build a stronger connection with them and ensure that they feel valued and appreciated. Consistency is not just about the frequency of your uploads, but also about the quality of your content. You should strive to create high-quality, engaging videos that resonate with your audience and provide value. This can involve researching and planning your content in advance, using high-quality equipment, and taking the time to edit and refine your videos.

Finally, it is important to be flexible and adaptable when it comes to your upload schedule. While it is important to maintain consistency, there may be times when you need to adjust your schedule due to unforeseen circumstances or changes in your personal or professional life. In such cases, it is important to communicate with your viewers and keep them updated on any changes to your upload schedule.

In summary, maintaining consistency with your upload schedule is crucial to building a successful

YouTube channel. This can involve establishing a regular upload schedule, maintaining consistency in the quality and format of your videos, engaging with your audience on a regular basis, creating high-quality content, and being flexible when necessary. By focusing on consistency, you can build a loyal following and achieve success on YouTube.

Chapter-4

Optimize your videos for search engines by using relevant keywords and tags.

Optimizing your YouTube videos for search engines can greatly increase your visibility and reach on the platform. By using relevant keywords and tags, you can help your videos to appear higher in search results, making them easier for viewers to find.

The first step in optimizing your videos is to conduct keyword research. This involves identifying the keywords and phrases that are most relevant to your video content and audience. You can use tools like Google Keyword Planner or YouTube's built-in search bar to find popular keywords and phrases that are related to your content.

Once you have identified your target keywords, you should include them in your video's title, description, and tags. This will help search engines understand what your video is about and increase its chances of appearing in relevant search results. However, it is important to use your keywords strategically and avoid keyword stuffing, which can actually harm your video's visibility and search rankings.

In addition to keywords, you should also use relevant tags to help categorize and organize your videos. Tags are like labels that help YouTube's algorithm to understand the content of your videos and suggest them to viewers who may be interested. You should use tags that accurately reflect the content of your video, including both broad and specific tags, and avoid using irrelevant or misleading tags.

Another important factor in optimizing your videos for search engines is to create high-quality, engaging content. Search engines take into account factors like watch time, engagement, and viewer retention when ranking videos, so it is important to create videos that are interesting, informative, and valuable to your audience. This can involve researching your audience and their interests, using a compelling thumbnail and title, and optimizing your video's length and pacing.

It is also important to promote your videos through social media and other channels to increase their visibility and reach. By sharing your videos on platforms like Twitter, Facebook, and Instagram, you can attract new viewers and increase engagement with your existing audience. You can also use paid promotion tools like YouTube Ads to reach a wider audience and increase your video's visibility.

Finally, you should regularly monitor and analyze your video's performance to understand what is working and what can be improved. You can use YouTube Analytics to track metrics like views, watch time, engagement, and retention, and make data-driven decisions about your content strategy. By constantly refining and optimizing your video content, you can increase your visibility and reach on YouTube and build a successful channel.

In summary, optimizing your YouTube videos for search engines involves conducting keyword research, using relevant keywords and tags, creating high-quality content, promoting your videos through social media and other channels, and regularly monitoring and analyzing your video's performance. By focusing on search engine optimization, you can increase your visibility and reach on YouTube and attract new viewers to your channel.

Chapter-5

Collaborate with other YouTubers in

your niche

To reach a wider audience .

Collaborating with other YouTubers in your niche can be an effective way to reach a wider audience and grow your channel. By working together, you can share your audiences and cross-promote each other's content, which can increase your visibility and engagement on the platform.

The first step in collaborating with other YouTubers is to identify potential partners who share your niche and target audience. This can involve researching other channels in your niche, attending industry events and conferences, and reaching out to other creators through social media and email. You should look for creators who have a similar style and audience to your own, and who are open to collaborating.

Once you have identified potential collaborators, you should reach out to them and propose a collaboration idea. This can involve creating a joint video, featuring each other's content in your videos, or participating in a challenge or event together. You should be clear about your goals and expectations for the collaboration, and be open to feedback and suggestions from your partner.

When collaborating with other YouTubers, it is important to be professional and respectful at all times. You should communicate clearly and consistently with your partner, and be flexible and accommodating to their needs and preferences. You should also be open to constructive criticism and feedback, and use it to improve your content and collaboration skills.

Another important factor in collaborating with other YouTubers is to promote the collaboration through your social media and other channels. By sharing teasers, behind-the-scenes footage, and other promotional materials, you can generate buzz and excitement around the collaboration, and attract new viewers to your channel. You should also cross-promote each other's channels and videos, and encourage your audiences to subscribe to each other's channels.

In addition to collaborating with other YouTubers, you can also participate in YouTube communities and forums to network with other creators and learn from their experiences. These communities can provide valuable resources and support and can help you to stay up-to-date with the latest trends and best practices in your niche.

Finally, you should regularly evaluate the success of your collaborations and adjust your strategy as needed. You can use YouTube Analytics and other tools to track metrics like views, engagement, and subscriber growth, and make data-driven decisions about your collaboration strategy. By constantly refining and optimizing your collaboration efforts, you can increase your reach and engagement on YouTube and build a successful channel.

In summary, collaborating with other YouTubers in your niche can be an effective way to reach a wider audience and grow your channel. This involves identifying potential partners, proposing a collaboration idea, being professional and respectful, promoting the collaboration through social media and other channels, participating in YouTube communities, and regularly evaluating the success of your collaborations. By focusing on collaboration, you can increase your visibility and engagement on YouTube and attract new viewers to your channel.

Chapter-6

Promote your videos on social media and other platforms to increase visibility.

Promoting your videos on social media and other platforms can be an effective way to increase their visibility and reach a wider audience. By leveraging the power of social media and other channels, you can drive traffic to your YouTube channel and boost engagement on your videos. The first step in promoting your videos on social media is to identify the platforms where your target audience is most active. This can involve researching social media trends and demographics and analyzing your own audience data on YouTube and other channels. You should focus on platforms that are popular among your target audience, and where you can share your videos in a way that is relevant and engaging. Once you have identified the platforms where you want to promote your videos, you should create a promotion strategy that is tailored to each platform. This can involve creating social media posts, blog articles, and other content that highlights your videos and encourages viewers to watch and engage with them. You should also use relevant hashtags and keywords to increase the visibility of your content and leverage the power of influencers and other thought leaders in your niche to amplify your message.

Another important factor in promoting your videos on social media is to be consistent and engaging with your audience. You should regularly post updates, respond to comments and questions, and share behind-the-scenes footage and other exclusive content that gives your audience a glimpse into your world. By building a strong relationship with your audience on social media, you can increase their loyalty and engagement with your brand, and ultimately drive more traffic to your YouTube channel.

In addition to social media, there are many other platforms and channels that you can use to promote your videos and increase their visibility. These can include email marketing, influencer marketing, paid advertising, and other forms of online marketing that can help you to reach a wider audience and drive more traffic to your channel. When promoting your videos on social media and other platforms, it is important to be strategic and data-driven in your approach. You should use analytics tools to track the performance of your promotions and make data-driven decisions about your marketing strategy based on the metrics that matter most to your channel. This can include metrics like views, engagement, click-through rates, and subscriber growth, which can help you to measure the success of your promotions and adjust your strategy as needed.

In summary, promoting your videos on social media and other platforms can be an effective way to increase their visibility and reach a wider audience. This involves identifying the platforms where your target audience is most active, creating a tailored promotion strategy for each platform, being consistent and engaging with your audience, and using data-driven metrics to evaluate the success of your promotions. By focusing on promotion, you can drive more traffic to your YouTube channel and boost engagement on your videos, which can ultimately help you to build a successful channel.

Chapter-7

Encourage your viewers to like, comment, and share

your videos to help them reach more people .

Encouraging your viewers to like, comment, and share your videos is an important part of building a successful YouTube channel. By engaging your viewers and encouraging them to interact with your content, you can help your videos reach more people and increase their engagement and visibility.

One of the most effective ways to encourage your viewers to like, comment, and share your videos is to create high-quality, engaging content that resonates with your audience. This can involve identifying the needs and interests of your target audience, and creating videos that address their pain points, answer their questions, and provide valuable insights and information.

Once you have created engaging content, you can encourage your viewers to like, comment, and share your videos by including calls to action in your videos and descriptions. This can involve asking your viewers to like your video if they enjoyed it, leaving a comment with their thoughts and feedback, and sharing the video with their friends and followers on social media.

Another effective way to encourage engagement and sharing is to create a sense of community around your channel. This can involve responding to comments and questions, hosting live streams and Q&A sessions, and creating social media groups or forums where your viewers can connect and engage with each other. By creating a sense of belonging and community around your channel, you can increase engagement and encourage your viewers to share your videos with their friends and followers.

In addition to these strategies, there are many other tactics that you can use to encourage engagement and sharing on your channel. These can include hosting giveaways and contests, collaborating with other YouTubers and influencers, and leveraging the power of paid advertising and other online marketing channels to increase the reach and visibility of your content.

Ultimately, the key to encouraging engagement and sharing on your channel is to focus on creating high-quality, engaging content that resonates with your audience. By understanding the needs and interests of your viewers, and creating content that addresses these needs in a unique and valuable way, you can build a loyal and engaged audience that is eager to like, comment, and share your videos with their friends and followers.

In summary, encouraging your viewers to like, comment, and share your videos is an important part of building a successful YouTube channel. This involves creating high-quality, engaging content that resonates with your audience, including calls to action in your videos and descriptions, creating a sense of community around your channel, and leveraging other tactics like giveaways, collaborations, and online marketing to increase the reach and visibility of your content. By focusing on engagement and sharing, you can help your videos reach more people and build a loyal and engaged audience that is eager to support your channel.

Chapter-8

Engage with your audience by responding to comments and messages, and listening to their feedback.

Engaging with your audience is a crucial part of building a successful YouTube channel. By responding to comments and messages, and listening to your viewers' feedback, you can create a sense of community and build a loyal following that is invested in your content. One of the most effective ways to engage with your audience is by responding to comments on your videos. This can involve thanking viewers for their comments, answering questions, and providing additional information or context about your videos.

By responding to comments, you can create a dialogue with your viewers and show them that you value their feedback and opinions.
In addition to responding to comments, it is important to actively seek out feedback from your viewers. This can involve creating polls or surveys to gather feedback on your content, or simply asking your viewers for their thoughts and opinions on specific topics. By listening to your viewers' feedback, you can gain valuable insights into what they like and don't like about your content, and use this information to improve your videos and grow your channel.
Another effective way to engage with your audience is by hosting live streams and Q&A sessions. This can involve setting aside time each week or month to answer your viewers' questions and interact with them in real time. By hosting live streams, you can create a sense of community and build a deeper connection with your viewers, while also providing them with valuable insights and information.
In addition to these tactics, there are many other ways to engage with your audience on YouTube.

For example, you can create social media groups or forums where your viewers can connect with each other and discuss your content, or collaborate with other YouTubers and influencers to reach new audiences and create engaging content. Ultimately, the key to engaging with your audience on YouTube is to be authentic, responsive, and genuinely interested in your viewers' feedback and opinions. By showing your viewers that you value their input and are committed to creating content that resonates with them, you can build a loyal following that is eager to support your channel and help it grow.

In summary, engaging with your audience on YouTube is a crucial part of building a successful channel. This involves responding to comments and messages, actively seeking out feedback from your viewers, hosting live streams and Q&A sessions, and using other tactics like social media groups and collaborations to connect with your audience. By being authentic, responsive, and genuinely interested in your viewers' feedback and opinions, you can build a loyal following that is invested in your content and eager to support your channel.

Chapter-9

Use eye-catching thumbnails and titles to attract viewers

and entice them to click on your videos .

In the highly competitive world of YouTube, one of the most effective ways to stand out from the crowd is by creating eye-catching thumbnails and titles. Thumbnails are the small images that appear next to your video title in search results and on your channel page. Titles are the headlines that appear above the thumbnail and provide a brief overview of the content of your video.

An eye-catching thumbnail is essential because it is the first thing viewers will see when they come across your video. It should be visually appealing, high-quality, and accurately represent the content of your video. Avoid using clickbait images that misrepresent your content, as this can lead to a loss of trust and credibility with your audience. The title of your video should also be engaging and informative. It should accurately reflect the content of your video and provide a clear idea of what viewers can expect to see. Keep your titles short and to the point, and use keywords that accurately reflect the content of your video.

To create effective thumbnails and titles, consider the following tips:

1. Use high-quality images: Your thumbnail should be visually appealing and high-quality. Use images that are clear and easy

to see, and avoid using images that are blurry or low-resolution.

2. Use bright and bold colors: Bright and bold colors can help your thumbnail stand out in a sea of search results. Use colors that are visually appealing and relevant to the content of your video.

3. Use text and graphics: Adding text or graphics to your thumbnail can help to provide additional context and entice viewers to click on your video. However, make sure that the text and graphics are easy to read and not too cluttered.

4. Keep your title short and to the point: Your title should be brief and to the point. Use keywords that accurately reflect the content of your video and make sure that your title is relevant to your audience.

5. Use numbers and lists: Using numbers and lists in your titles can help to make them more engaging and informative. For example, "10 Tips for Creating Eye-Catching Thumbnails" or "5 Ways to Grow Your YouTube Channel."

6. Use emotional triggers: Using emotional triggers in your titles can help to make them more engaging and memorable. For example, "How to Overcome Your Fear of Public Speaking" or "Why You Should Start Your Own Business Today."

In conclusion, using eye-catching thumbnails and titles is essential for attracting viewers to your videos and standing out in a crowded field. By using high-quality images, bright colors, text, and graphics, keeping your titles short and to the point, and using numbers and emotional triggers, you can create engaging and effective thumbnails and titles that entice viewers to click on your videos. By doing so, you can increase your visibility on YouTube, grow your audience, and ultimately achieve success on the platform.

Chapter-10

Stay up-to-date with trends and changes in the YouTube algorithm to stay ahead of the competition .

YouTube is constantly evolving, and it's important to stay up-to-date with the latest trends and changes in the platform's algorithm if you want to stay ahead of the competition. The YouTube algorithm is a complex system that determines which videos are recommended to users, based on factors such as watch time, engagement, and relevance. By understanding how the algorithm works and keeping up with the latest trends, you can optimize your videos and increase your chances of success on the platform.

Here are some tips for staying up-to-date with trends and changes in the YouTube algorithm:

1. Follow YouTube's Creator Insider channel: This channel provides updates on the latest changes to the YouTube algorithm, as well as tips and best practices for creators.

2. Attend YouTube conferences and events: YouTube hosts a variety of conforonoco and events for creators throughout the year. Attending these events can help you stay up-to-date on the latest trends and changes in the platform, as well as network with other creators.

3. Follow YouTube news outlets and blogs: There are several news outlets and blogs that cover the latest trends and changes in the YouTube world, such as TubeFilter and The Verge.

4. Use analytics tools to track your performance: Analytics tools like YouTube Studio can provide insights into how your videos are performing and which factors are driving engagement. Use these tools to track your performance and identify areas for improvement.

5. Experiment with new formats and trends: The YouTube algorithm rewards creators who are innovative and willing to experiment with new formats and trends. Keep an eye on what's popular in your niche and try to incorporate these trends into your content.

6. Stay on top of changes in your niche: Trends and changes in your specific niche can also impact your success on YouTube. Keep an eye on what your competitors are doing, and stay up-to-date on the latest news and developments in your industry.

7. Engage with your audience: Engaging with your audience is not only a great way to build a loyal following, but it can also help you stay up-to-date with the latest trends and changes in the platform. Pay attention to the comments on your videos and respond to feedback from your audience.

In conclusion, staying up-to-date with trends and changes in the YouTube algorithm is essential for success on the platform. By following YouTube's Creator Insider channel, attending conferences and events, following YouTube news outlets and blogs, using analytics tools, experimenting with new formats and trends, staying on top of changes in your niche, and engaging with your audience, you can stay ahead of the competition and achieve success on the platform.

Chapter-11

Build a strong brand identity and use it consistently
across all your social media

<u>platforms</u> .

When it comes to building a successful YouTube channel, having a strong brand identity is essential. Your brand identity is how you present yourself and your content to the world, and it includes everything from your channel name and logo to the type of content you produce and the tone of your voice. By creating a strong brand identity and using it consistently across all your social media platforms, you can establish yourself as a recognizable and trusted source of content on YouTube.

Here are some tips for building a strong brand identity on YouTube:

1. Define your niche and target audience: Before you can build a strong brand identity, you need to have a clear understanding of your niche and target audience. Who are you creating content for, and what kind of content are they interested in? By defining your niche and target audience, you can tailor your content and messaging to resonate with them.

2. Choose a channel name and logo that reflects your brand: Your channel name and logo should be memorable and reflective of your brand identity. Choose a name and logo that are easy to remember and visually appealing.

3. Develop a consistent visual identity: Consistency is key when it comes to building a strong brand identity. Develop a consistent visual identity across all your social media platforms, including your YouTube channel, by using the same colors, fonts, and design elements.

4. Establish a tone of voice: Your tone of voice should reflect your brand personality and be consistent across all your content. Are you informative and authoritative, or are you more casual and humorous? Establish a tone of voice that aligns with your brand identity and resonates with your audience.

5. Create high-quality, consistent content: Your content is a reflection of your brand, so it's important to create high-quality, consistent content that aligns with your brand identity. Use your brand identity as a guide when creating new content, and make sure that all your content is on-brand and aligned with your messaging.

6. Use social media to build your brand: Social media is a powerful tool for building your brand and reaching a wider audience. Use social media to promote your content and engage with your audience, and make sure that your branding is consistent across all your social media platforms.

7. Collaborate with other creators: Collaborating with other creators in your

niche is a great way to expand your reach and build your brand. Choose collaborators whose brand identity aligns with yours, and create content together that reflects both of your brands.

In conclusion, building a strong brand identity is essential for success on YouTube. By defining your niche and target audience, choosing a channel name and logo that reflects your brand, developing a consistent visual identity, establishing a tone of voice, creating high-quality, consistent content, using social media to build your brand, and collaborating with other creators, you can establish yourself as a recognizable and trusted source of content on YouTube.

Chapter-12

Use analytics to track your performance and make data-driven decisions to improve your channel .

Using analytics to track your performance is a crucial aspect of building a successful YouTube channel. YouTube offers a wealth of data and insights that can help you understand your audience, track your progress, and make data-driven decisions to improve your content and grow your channel.

One of the most important metrics to track is your watch time, which is the total amount of time that viewers spend watching your videos. This is a key factor in YouTube's algorithm, as it prioritizes videos that have high watch times and engagement rates. You can use analytics to identify which videos have the highest watch times and engagement rates and use this information to guide your content strategy.

Another important metric is your audience retention, which measures how long viewers stay engaged with your videos. You can use this information to identify which parts of your videos are most engaging, and which parts may be causing viewers to drop off. This can help you make targeted improvements to your content to keep viewers engaged and increase your watch time.

You should also track your subscriber growth over time, as this can help you understand how your channel is growing and identify any trends or patterns. You can use analytics to see which videos are driving the most subscribers, and use this information to create more content that resonates with your audience.

In addition to these metrics, YouTube analytics also provides valuable information about your audience demographics, including age, gender, location, and interests. You can use this information to better understand your audience and tailor your content to their preferences.

To make the most of YouTube analytics, it's important to regularly review your data and use it to make informed decisions about your content strategy. For example, if you notice that certain types of videos consistently have high watch times and engagement rates, you may want to focus more on creating similar content in the future. Alternatively, if you notice that certain videos have low watch times or engagement rates, you may want to consider making changes to your content or promoting those videos more heavily to boost their performance.

In addition to YouTube's built-in analytics, there are also third-party tools available that can provide more detailed insights into your channel's performance. These tools can help you track your progress over time, compare your performance to competitors, and identify new opportunities for growth.

Ultimately, using analytics to track your performance is a crucial part of building a successful YouTube channel. By understanding your audience, monitoring your progress, and making data-driven decisions, you can continuously improve your content and grow your channel over time.

Chapter-13

Experiment with different types of content to see what   resonates with your audience .

Experimenting with different types of content is an essential part of creating a successful YouTube channel. Not all types of content will resonate with your audience, and it's essential to find what works best for you and your audience.

Here are some tips for experimenting with different types of content:

1. Analyze your audience: Start by analyzing your audience to determine what types of content they are interested in. Look at your YouTube analytics to identify your most popular videos and the demographics of your viewers. Use this information to inform your content experimentation.

2. Try different formats: Experiment with different video formats, such as tutorials, reviews, vlogs, interviews, and more. Mix up your content to keep things fresh and engaging for your audience. You can also try combining different formats to create unique content.

3. Collaborate with other creators: Collaborating with other creators in your niche is an excellent way to experiment with

new types of content. It can help you reach new audiences and expose you to new content ideas.

4. Listen to feedback: Pay attention to the comments and feedback you receive from your viewers. This feedback can help you understand what types of content your audience enjoys and what they want to see more of. Use this feedback to inform your future content experimentation.

5. Test and iterate: Test different types of content and iterate based on the results. If a particular type of content performs well, try creating more of it. If it doesn't perform well, try a different approach. The key is to keep experimenting and refining your content strategy over time.

In conclusion, experimenting with different types of content is a crucial part of building a successful YouTube channel. It can help you find what works best.

Chapter-14

Create a community around your channel by hosting live streams and interact with your viewers in real-time .

Creating a community around your YouTube

channel is an excellent way to build a loyal following and grow your audience. Live streams are an effective tool for engaging with your viewers in real time and fostering a sense of community.

Here are some tips for hosting successful live streams and interacting with your viewers:

1. Plan your live streams: Plan your live streams in advance and promote them on your social media platforms and in your video descriptions. This will give your viewers plenty of notice and ensure that you have a good turnout.

2. Choose the right platform: Choose a live-streaming platform that is user-friendly and has the features you need. YouTube has its own built-in live-streaming feature, which is convenient for YouTubers.

3. Interact with your viewers: Engage with your viewers by answering their questions, responding to their comments, and acknowledging their presence. Encourage them to participate by asking them to share their thoughts or ideas.

4. Provide value: Make sure that your live streams provide value to your viewers. Consider sharing exclusive content, offering behind-the-scenes access, or hosting Q&A sessions.

5. Use live streams for collaborations: Live streams are an excellent way to collaborate

with other creators in your niche. Consider hosting joint live streams to reach new audiences and build relationships with other creators.

6. Monitor the chat: Monitor the chat during your live stream to ensure that the conversation remains respectful and on-topic. Use moderation tools to block or remove users who are behaving inappropriately.

7. Follow up after the live stream: Follow up with your viewers after the live stream to thank them for attending and to provide additional resources or information related to the stream's topic.

In conclusion, live streams are an excellent way to engage with your viewers in real time and build a sense of community around your channel. By following these tips, you can create successful live streams that provide value to your viewers and help you grow your audience.

Chapter-15

Monetize your channel by joining the YouTube Partner

The program, selling merchandise, or partnering

with

<u>sponsors</u> .

Monetizing your YouTube channel is an excellent way to turn your passion for creating videos into a source of income. There are several ways to monetize your channel, including joining the YouTube Partner Program, selling merchandise, and partnering with sponsors.
Here are some tips for monetizing your channel:

1. Join the YouTube Partner Program: To join the YouTube Partner Program, you need to meet the eligibility criteria, which include having at least 1,000 subscribers and 4,000 watch hours in the last 12 months. Once you join, you can monetize your videos with ads and earn revenue from the views.

2. Sell merchandise: Selling merchandise is an excellent way to monetize your channel while providing your viewers with branded products that they will love. Consider creating merchandise that is related to your niche or brand, such as t-shirts, stickers, or phone cases.

3. Partner with sponsors: Partnering with sponsors is an excellent way to monetize your channel while promoting products or services that are relevant to your audience. Make sure that any products or services that you promote align with your brand and add value to your viewers.

4. Use affiliate marketing: Affiliate marketing is another way to monetize your channel by promoting products or services and earning a commission on any sales that are made through your unique affiliate link.

5. Create sponsored content: Creating sponsored content is a great way to monetize your channel while promoting products or services that align with your brand. Make sure that any sponsored content you create is authentic and provides value to your viewers.

6. Offer premium content: Consider offering premium content, such as exclusive videos or behind-the-scenes access, to your viewers for a fee. This is an excellent way to monetize your channel while providing your viewers with additional value.

7. Use crowdfunding: Crowdfunding is another way to monetize your channel by allowing your viewers to support you directly. Consider using platforms such as Patreon or Ko-fi to offer exclusive content or rewards to your supporters.

In conclusion, monetizing your YouTube channel is an excellent way to turn your passion for creating videos into a source of income. By joining the YouTube Partner Program, selling merchandise, partnering with sponsors, using affiliate marketing, creating sponsored content, offering premium content, or using crowdfunding, you can monetize your channel in a way that works best for you and your audience.

www.ingramcontent.com/pod-product-compliance
Lightning Source LLC
Chambersburg PA
CBHW070904220526
45466CB00005B/2121

* 9 7 9 8 3 9 3 3 8 3 6 0 2 *